Here For What Matters
[Poems]

by Dr. Joanie Terrizzi

The following pages contain poems written during 2021 for all of us who are here for what matters. For more poems and information visit https://www.facebook.com/drjtpoetry

My dog
ate several baby rabbits
last night.

I heard a young
tender thing
screaming for its life
between his jaws
and I resonated with that part of me
that sometimes yearns
for my own vibrancy
that strongly.

I pulled him from his prey
grossed out and a little upset,
and totally at peace:
both the yearning for life
and the ending of life
have their place
in all this unfolding.

Knowing how many mountains
my friend has climbed
increased the sweetness
of watching him bestow
a beautiful name
upon the daughter
his heart has been
waiting for.

He named her for the forest,
and from across the room
I could feel the trees
calling to me –
and the mountains –
the air clean and bright
as the sweet baby's eyes.

We all climb
so.
many.
mountains.
to meet those
that are calling to us.

The night air
on my skin.

Oh, how divine
to have skin
that feels.

All of a sudden
(several years later)
I found myself in the midst
of a situation
that would have once wrought
the icy, shattering discomfort
left in my mind and heart
by the words and actions
of a frigid-hearted other.

It took me a minute
(all of a sudden)
to notice the absence of
the spike in heartbeat,
the racing thoughts,
the queasy stomach,
the plea of my being;
as absences are harder to notice
than presences.

Ah, what beautiful absence.
What fallow space
to fill with whatever I want.

What healing: so subtle
I might not have noticed it.
What freedom: to shed the
residue left behind by one so cold.
What gratitude: to live with
a heart warm enough to melt
what was never meant to be mine.

If you only knew
how loving humans could be
when they sit together
and listen patiently,
how could you go back
to the old way?

Why would you skate
on the frozen surface
when you know how warm
we all are underneath?

I can't unknow
how tender
the human heart is.
And I wouldn't want to.

In a shattered season
I watched a woman
I shared a traveling room with,
rubbing lotion
into her hands and feet
before bed.

I thought to myself,
"Wow, what tenderness.
I can see how much
she loves herself."

At the time I was
caught in the chasm
between myself and
my own love,
hearing neither clearly.

Now, several years later,
I find myself
rubbing lotion
into my hands and feet
before bed.

Wow, what tenderness.
I can see how much
I love myself.

Take sips of light
with your eyes.

This is yet another
definition
of being alive.

What sheer delight,
to be able
to drink light
with your eyes.

Some truths are so true
I would know them
a thousand lifetimes from now
in a dark room.

And sometimes
that's not enough.

Sometimes the sun
on my skin
in the garden
is far truer.

Of course you like having
your hands in the dirt,
you – all of you –
borne of the Earth
and knowing that
you eat from her
all the days of your breathing.

Of course your heart breaks
for the soil and the water
and the clouds and the air,
and the fragile plants
that do not grow.

Of course you know
with all your tender heart
that which was not tended.
And of course you know
the ache of a seed
that never met the sun.

It is no surprise that
the dirt under your fingernails
reminds you that
breathing and aliveness
are not one and the same
and that roots that know
their freedom in the darkness
bloom in the light
that sees them.

You doubt your ability
to believe in things
you cannot see.

Until you remember the wind,
and how even the
slightest breeze stroking
tree branches stirs you.

And then you remember love,
and how even the
slightest ounce alters
absolutely everything.

And you feel again your ability
to believe in the unseen
as even the slightest expression
of mystery presses itself
upon your experience.

At least for a breath
or two.

I saw a house with
the exact same front door
that my grandparents had
when I was a child.

And suddenly, I was
half my height and
a fraction of my age
staring up at that door,

and I would give anything
for that door to open
and to be enveloped into
the endlessly bright
pool of love that was always,
always,
on the other side of that door.

Returning to the familiar
(even the thrillingly new familiar)
no longer serves the heart's unfolding.

It's those wild, dark corners where I
might have mist, the places I cannot see.

It's the ability to be
nose-to-nose with my own fears.

It is meeting the walls inside
myself, trembling at what
might be on the other side,

and walking resolutely (trembling)
through what holds me back,
dismantling the wall between my heart
and the space into which I can unfold

and find out just how much is there.

Like a tuning fork
humming to herself
all her days

who hears a sound
so familiar, she feels
like she is listening
to her very bones.

Ah, this is resonance
she whispers to herself
knowing her own knowing

long after
it turns invisible.

All the things that are not
happening in my life are
not meant to be happening.

I know this because:
they are not happening.

The means of life
are not in the *meant to*,
they are in the *meaning*.

And regardless of how subtle or
preferable it may or may not be,

all the meaning is right *here*
in what *is* happening.

When you can see
the end of all
those you love,

when you can imagine
a world without them,
dim of their light,

how can you not love
with all the brightness
you can muster?

How can you not savor
the mundane with all the
fierceness of your heart?

Full moon:

Thank you for
reminding me to
turn my face
toward all the
light I can,

and that when I
reflect a face
full of light
I can illuminate
the way for those
who wander
in the dark,

whether or not
I myself
am radiant.

Life doesn't owe you
any love -

whether you were raised
in an ocean of love
or the desert of it -

no matter how parched
your lips are,

no matter how warm
your tattered heart is,

no matter how *good*
you have been –

Love simply shines
when she shines.

The final accounting
will never show that
I did not show up
with my whole heart.

It will never show
that this tender, scarred,
fiercely beating drum
in my breast

rested in her cage
when she could show up
with eighty-two batches
of tender bravery,

because it never happened.

This heart, so devoted
to my freedom and aliveness
is willing to fail
a thousand times

just to learn from love.

"Thank you for making it
mean something," he said,

and I startled.

In that moment
I remembered *myself*.

I felt – for the first time
in a whole yawn of time –
the lit-up cells in
this heart and mind,
the fabric of this soul
that was made

to make it mean something.

You, carrying the weight
of the entire world
in the cage of your ribs,
still thinking that
this is a problem.

But I ask you –
how could you
consider yourself alive
and not feel the weight
of this precious,
aching world?

This, too, is proof
of your aliveness –
what a splendid joy
to ache like this.

Oh, what depths an
experience carves in me.

I will never be the same
as I was before I wandered
in and out of this story.

And I wouldn't want to be.

I learned how to reclaim
my power.

I am harvesting the fruits
of my strength right now.

And my, are they delicious.

This miraculous bag
of breath and bones
that carries me over
ruts and cobblestones
rivers and mountains
terrors and dreams
carries me

home.

I have learned that
I cannot hold onto water -
unless it is ice -
and I would not want to.

My life is not that
cold and frozen (anymore).

What flows away, flows away.

Ach, you are so beautiful,
watching you flow down river
with floating leaves
and twirling twigs
knowing that no matter
how stunning you are

you're already gone.

Oh, sweet honesty:
your fruit that is
always ripe.

That gift I can give
to myself, always.

What ruthless and
deeply gratifying
wonder, to be right
up against **what is**
without any resistance.

It is my belief in the impossible
that allowed me to see far beyond
the confines of narrowness

to all that was possible if given
light and air and sustenance
and breath.

But possibilities wither
when they are not seen.

And even still, I would rather
live beyond the possible and
make my life miraculous.

Grateful to the tree
whose branches reached
for the sun, whose life
became my table.

Grateful to the hands
that tended earth and
soil and seedling and
harvest to bring
my food home to me.

Grateful for the
breath in my lungs
song in my heart
sun in my hair while
I cook my food.

Grateful every day to
those who truly *want*
to sit next to me
at the table.

Are you being who
you were born to be,
or are you hiding in the
shadow of yourself -

hoping that huge shadow
will not disclose
the enormous space
between you and the
eminence you were born to be?

What huge, gulping, vacuous
space – what wild, groundless,
incandescent space.

I will not tell anyone that
you are too afraid to
fall into the luminescence
of yourself to emerge from
the small corner inhabit –
even though I see you there.

When you are invisible
you can soak in all the
treasures of the world
without anyone noticing.

The patterns of leaf veins,
the last lick of sunset,
mycelium traversing undergrowth,
the horizon kissing the sky,
the ache of a broken tree
becoming what it is to be next.

And one day you might find,
with decades in your
discarded heart that
it has become as vast and
as breathtaking as
the star-twinkled sky.

No one gets to
rewrite your story,
taking out all the
parts where you shine.

You shine because
you are a breather
on this planet.

Breathing with the
heartbeat beings
and with the
root-and-leaf beings.

And anyone whose eyes
choose not to see that
lives as if
holding their breath.

"You should be happy," they say,
"Why do you dwell in the darkness?"

I am willing to be fully immersed in
my life, when it brings darkness and
when it brings light.

Being willing to sit in the dark
when it is dark has taught me that
I can make light with my bare hands.

The kind of light that dances
darkness back from whence it
came and lights my way.

And I can hope that any bit
that spills as I dance might
light the way for others.

I cannot think of any deeper
happiness than this.

Yesterday I validated
two friends who have
grieved deeply.

It really *is* that heavy.

Even [especially] when you
hide it away to protect
all those who don't understand.

And oh, the exhaustion of doing
origami with your soul
to constantly make it
into the shape of
not being needy
just to be small enough
to fit into the world.

It really *is* that exhausting.

All the light you're
looking for
is in your heart.

And you can light another
candle every night.
Ach, how bright it is.

But for goodness' sake,
clear the way,
open the curtains,
move the furniture
out of the way

and let all that light
get out.

There is very little
I can imagine
to remind me what is
truly important
like watching a husband
wipe the chin
of his dying beloved.

Here's to the precarious and
delicate stacks of our lives
on which set our hearts so that
we can go on with our living.

Some of us believing the stack to
be solid, holding our hearts safe,

others knowing emphatically that
there is no stack where we perceive
it to be, just the free-falling
heart, fully alive.

Each breath alters *everything*; the
heart aware of its own aliveness
can never be set on perceived safety,
every moment achingly beautiful:

subtle, delicate, ephemeral.